THE YEAR BOSTON WON THE PENNANT

THE YEAR BOSTON
WON THE PENNANT

JOHN FORD NOONAN

GROVE PRESS, INC.
NEW YORK

IN HONOR OF

BILLY CHESBORO (MOST OF ALL)
FRAN DRISCOLL
RAYMOND JOHN PETER BARRY, JR.
PUCCI MOLINA
CHUCK BERRY
SISTER MARY FELICITAS
DOCTOR JOHN & RITA MOTHER
PAUL ROSENFELS
KAYE STEVENSON
S. PAUL KASHAP
FOGG CANNON (OUT OF
WOONSOCKET)
BUBBLES LAHR AND IMPOSSIBLE
POPE JOHN XXIII
GRETCHEN EFFLER (LEAST OF ALL)
MARCIA AND HER CHILDREN
SAVOY BROWN BAND
POLICEMEN
ARIEL
UNCLE RANSOM AND VERA
FILLMORE FAMILY (EXCEPT KEVAN)
A. J. MEROVICK AND LAURA AND
JENNIE
UNCLE BOB McGANNON

AND

RENALDE GUISEPPE VICENTE CUCCIA
D. E. BYRD AND THE HERD
WOLFGANG GRAJONCA
EVELYN KILBOURNE AND SAM
ROPER THE WRITER
STEVE ABRAMS
RALPH McCARTNEY
BIG JULES ESTABLISHMENT (ISRAEL)
THE REAL STANLEY KUCKTA
THE ONE AND ONLY R. C. CHURCH
BIG ROY AND CYNTHIA THE BELLE
HERB BRAHA'S FINGERS
CICELY NICHOLS
CHIEF AND MINNIE McGANNON
RIVIERA GEORGE
TUNES TUNICK, DOC, WELLS AND SHERMAN
PAT NIXON'S DICK

THE YEAR BOSTON WON THE PENNANT was presented by Jules Irving at the Forum Theatre in Lincoln Center, New York City, on May 22, 1969, with the following cast:

DILLINGER, MINIVER PEABODY,
    2ND MAN .... Lenny Baker
SHATTUCK, LEROY STARR .... Jerome Dempsey
KOLKOWSKI, MICROPHONE TECHNICIAN,
    1ST DELIVERY MAN .... Ronald Schaeffer
O'CONNOR, 2ND DELIVERY MAN,
    OLIVARE FRISCH .... Joseph Schroer
STANLEY KUCKTA, JASPER TERHUNE,
    GEORGE .... Paul Benjamin
JOJO DELORENZO, TUCKER LURTSEMA,
    GROUNDSKEEPER AT FENWAY
    PARK .... Ralph Drischell
MARCUS SYKOWSKI .... Roy R. Scheider
MAN IN A RAINCOAT .... William Myers
JULIAN LA MONDE, OSCAR .... Richard Woods
CANDY CANE SYKOWSKI ...... Marcia Jean Kurtz
MARTHA PEABODY, LAVERNE JONES, 3RD
    WOMAN IN PARTY SCENE .... Marilyn Sokol
PEPPER WEITZ, 1ST WOMAN IN PARTY
    SCENE .... Jane Altman
2ND WOMAN IN PARTY SCENE .... Joan Jeffri

THE YEAR BOSTON WON THE PENNANT

1

Speaker at the Country Club

Backstage center a bench, long and bare. Seven men sit on it, faces expressionless, waiting. Stage-left end of bench, a one-armed man, Marcus Sykowski. He wears a "Boston Red Sox" warm-up jacket. Downstage left, an orange-painted loudspeaker socketed to the proscenium frame. Prolonged silence, 10 seconds, 20 . . .

LOUDSPEAKER VOICE *(barking)* : Good morning, boys. It's your happy Fatman speaking. Got enough golf bags out here for everybody. Grass green, sun hot and creamy . . . so it's time to walk and talk, shag and bag. O.K. now, Stanley Kuckta . . . on 2 and 19; O'Connor . . . on 31 and 40; and Kolkowski . . . on 88 and 90.

THREE MEN *rise and disappear offstage.*

Shattuck . . . on 3 and 79; Dillinger, our boy with the twelve-inch stinger . . . on 7 and 17.

TWO MEN *rise and begin to cross.*

DILLINGER: How come they don't call the guy with the one arm first? He's always the earliest one here.

SHATTUCK (*slapping* DILLINGER *hard in the head*) : **Don't** you know who that is, stupid?

TWO MEN disappear, leaving one-armed MARCUS SYKOWSKI *and older man* JOJO DELORENZO *at opposite ends of the bench.* MARCUS *reaches under bench and pulls out a weighted bag. Holding it by strap, he begins set of bicep exercises with intact arm. He completes exercise set. Deep breath, a smile, then onto second set. Tempo increased, smile grows. Pushing arm to limit, bag loudly dropped, sigh of exhaustion.*

DELORENZO: Kid, you pull it a lot? Read once guys lift weights pull it a lot? (*Pause.*) Whack, whack, whack, ha, ha, ha! (*Slapping leg, laughing to self. Suddenly opens old and dirt-stained newspaper, turning to back page.*) Got your picture splattered all over the back page, kid. One of them color photo blast-ups, bigger than life and just like you look now. Why, if I was worshipped, a national legendary, I sure wouldn't end up back here!

LOUDSPEAKER VOICE: O.K., Sykowski . . . 34!

MARCUS *drops exercise bag, begins to run off.* LOUDSPEAKER VOICE *suddenly quiet and respectful.*

Mr. Sykowski, be patient with us. We have to find you something lighter . . .

MARCUS *crosses back to bench.*

DELORENZO: Maybe when you lose both arms, they'll call you first . . .

LOUDSPEAKER VOICE: Capote . . . on 37 and 50.

DELORENZO (*yelling loudly*) : Not here!

LOUDSPEAKER VOICE: JoJo Delorenzo, you want it?

DELORENZO (*more loudly*) : Forget it!

LOUDSPEAKER VOICE: JoJo Delorenzo, you having a good time today?

DELORENZO (*screaming*) : Up yours! (*Reading from inside paper.*) Says here Red Sox gave you 75 Gs to sign in '61. Says last two years you were highest paid pitcher in the game, saying faster than Feller or Koufax you were. Says Boston mighta won the flag this year you hadn't disappeared in the heat of the race . . . Man, who's kidding who! Boston, they couldn't win playing a can of turds! (*Returning to back page.*) Some set of bouncers the wife got . . . and there's a Marcus Junior, too! (*Pause.*) Why'd you never say to me you had a kid? (*Reading on.*) Story don't explain how you lost the arm!

MARCUS *starts another set of exercises with weighted bag.*

They must be kiddin' about the comeback crap! Who ever heard of a one-arm pitcher?

MARCUS SYKOWSKI (*continuing exercise, staring straight ahead*) : Grover Pepperidge, Southern League, '31 to '37, won 177 games . . .

DELORENZO: Bet this Grover guy never made it to the big leagues? (*No response, JoJo jumping up from bench.*) Knew I was right, can't be done . . . (*Pause.*) Got a dumbbell in there, don't you? (*Pause.*) Story don't explain how you lost the

3

arm. (*Pause.*) Know goddamn well there's a dumb-bell in there, don't be embarrassed. So you take the thing out of the bag and let's see it! (*Rubbing hands and arms vigorously.*) Story don't explain what the wife does?

MARCUS: She's an actress.

DELORENZO: Well then, what are you doing here?

MARCUS: She acts . . .

LOUDSPEAKER VOICE: Capote . . . on 37 and 50.

DELORENZO: Not here!

LOUDSPEAKER VOICE: Mr. Sykowski, pretty soon we'll have something nice and light . . .

DELORENZO (*continuing to rub hands and arms*) : Pretty cold for November, huh? (*Wetting index finger, holding it up to the air.*) A strong breeze . . . coming straight from the north-south!

MARCUS: Yes . . .

DELORENZO: Ha! Ha! Ha! Don't you get it? Ha, ha, ha, *north-south,* can't be! Kid, 75 Gs from the great Gold Sox of Boston, best chucker in the game, and you can't even tell when I feed you something that can't be. (*Circling* MARCUS.) You know, you fall from the big stuff, you ain't shit no more, you hear me, nothing—same as us! You that embarrassed about being here, you drag your ass the hell out. (*In fury dives at* MARCUS, *embracing him about legs.*) What am I gunna tell my Momma? Remember the snapper pond on number 13, smashing the turtles' heads, and when you took a crap in Mrs. Ferguson's golf bag the 4th of July in '53, and the time you handed the visiting tournament golf pro the golfball of soap and how it exploded all over. The stories, they're so many, over and over I feed 'em to her and Momma, eighty, can hardly walk, she screams, "You're nothing, nothing, nothing but a liar!" I known you since you was small as a colt and then I . . . Come on, how'd you ever blow the 75 Gs, what about what you made last year? And how come the management ain't supporting you, I mean, you're famous? Kid, come on, I gotta have something good to tell Momma, else . . . this is crazy! Didn't you even have insurance? (*Letting* MARCUS *go, taking out handkerchief, blowing nose loudly.*) I'm your old buddy. I hope to God I didn't hurt your arm more!

MARCUS (*placing his hand warmly on JoJo's head, smiling widely*) : If they send me out once a day and twice Saturdays and Sundays till the snow comes, that'll be just enough to buy myself a chrome arm that operates off nerve impulses, the newest thing, came out just last year. Nothing happened to my pitching arm which I'm making stronger than ever with this lifting . . . so if I can maneuver the chrome piece by spring, then I can hook my glove to it and I'll be fine! (*Laughing to self.*) One-arm Grover Pepperidge made it with nothing but a hunk of wood. . . .

DELORENZO: Whatever made you come back?

MARCUS (*attention suddenly drawn offstage, fearfully two steps backwards*) : I have to go now! (*Crossing to bench, putting weighted bag under it.*) And I thought I was through with them people!

DELORENZO: Kid, what's the matter, why do you keep lookin' over there? (*Rushing to* MARCUS.) Do you know the guy? Listen, I'll lend you five you're in trouble . . .

MARCUS: Remember Joe Bremm, used to caddy with us? Just remembered he still owes me twenty bucks. Gunna pay old Joe a visit . . . (*Bolting offstage.*) Watch my weights for me. I'll be back tomorrow.

A few seconds and a MAN IN A RAINCOAT *appears.*

DELORENZO: Listen, sport, I don't know who you are, but you're not wanted back here, O.K.!

MAN IN RAINCOAT: Hey you! Have any idea where Sy . . . Sy . . . (*From out of breast pocket, a piece of paper; he reads it.*) Where *Sykronski's* aimed?

DELORENZO: Name's *Sykowski,* sport, the great *Sykowski!* Why you want to know, you a newspaper guy?

MAN IN RAINCOAT: Have any idea where he's aimed?

DELORENZO: Listen, sport, you'd better blow before . . . 'cause you're not wanted back here, understand?

MAN *follows after* MARCUS *offstage.*

LOUDSPEAKER VOICE: Capote . . . on 37 and 50!

DELORENZO: Not here!

LOUDSPEAKER VOICE: Tell Sykowski pretty soon we'll have something nice and light!

DELORENZO (*rushes back to bench. With one arm tries to lift weighted bag but cannot*): He's gunna do it . . . gunna make it back with a metal arm. He told me so himself!

LOUDSPEAKER VOICE: Capote, where are you . . . on 37 and 50!

DELORENZO: I'll take it . . . (*Struggling, he lifts bag with both arms. Running offstage, bag in arms, jumping, yelling.*) Oh Momma, Momma, Momma, whataya got to say to me now!

2

In the Fall of the Year

Julian La Monde's apartment. MARCUS *and middle-aged distinguished man,* LA MONDE, *appear upstage center, crossing down.*

JULIAN LA MONDE: I don't read the sports section of newspapers, but I have heard of you, Marcus Sykowski. Oh, have I, have I indeed!

MARCUS: Sir, my wife'll wonder where I am . . .

LA MONDE: But wonder what she'll wonder . . . wondering! (*Into breast pocket, a handful of money, giving it to* MARCUS.) There, good Marcus, one hundred lovely dollars . . . (MARCUS, *passionate counting of gift.*) Aren't you going to say thank you?

MARCUS: Joe Bremm only owed me twenty bucks, but can I use the extra dough! Thanks, Mr. La Monde, you're some fella!

MARCUS *starts upstage. Several steps,* LA MONDE *charging after, grabbing him.*

LA MONDE: Good Marcus, no, no, you mustn't . . . not yet!

MARCUS: It's getting dark and I——

LA MONDE: Just one tiny favor, please, take but a whisper of time!

MARCUS: A whisper? Sure!

LA MONDE: Good Marcus, tomorrow a book of my poems
is to be released in all the local stores. For tomorrow
I've waited all my life and tomorrow is now upon us!
(*Withdrawing book from hip pocket.*) It's called
The Velvet Spoon! As you may or may not know, I
also authored *Leonard Is a Name for Roses.* Unfor-
tunately, *Leonard* was judged too personal for gen-
eral publication and so was distributed in limited
Xerox editions in certain delicate circles in and
around Brookline. Sadly, I haven't a copy here, so
from my penultimate work, the opening eulogy of
The Velvet Spoon: (*reading*) "In the fall of the
• year, the few noticedly uncared-for trees of our great
city yield, open forth, their wombs plied by that
ravenous rapist called . . . Winter. Yes, submit,
emit their librous leaves that leap pell-mell, dive,
spin for a cavernous death into the soup of feet far
below, becoming a grounded hodgepodge of dead
cigarette butts and Lifesaver wrappers that are nothing but sadly remounted prophylactics, all to become
gelatinous sweetness in the wake of a thick autumn
rain. Oh, in the fall of the year, this year, the one
true season of any year, diverse acts of sad descension
proliferate like mad colonies of undiaphragmed
crabs! Oh, in the fall of the year, much, so, so, so
much, much falls."

MARCUS: Sir, my wife worries when I miss supper!

LA MONDE: No, no, please. At this juncture I reach my
inspirational peak! (*Reading on.*) ". . . Picture in
your mind if you may the Upper Back Bay Drive,

North Charles River . . . an archetypal of strewn steel riveted nattily in angel wings, a fabrous weave of Western dream, a ghettoed harvest of plasticity borne high by virtue of prolixity, oh, give your best eye! See a woman, mid-forty, wend her way, waltz waddlingly, her aim the johnny room, her skin paper thin and out of print, daffy-cracked, lines of blaring blue. Yet she prances nimbly for friends swear, 'For your age, Dearie, you're a leopard incarnate, and graced of such sweet crotch.' " Sweet crotch, and so near a tasty phrase! "Give us a wall stretched mirror and Madam within it, staring eyes, breasts belly-bent, the nips . . ." (*Suddenly stopping.*) Oh, good Marcus, why do I always go too far, illumine too much, why? Yes, yes, an ode to yourself, a piece improvised: "Good Marcus S., munificently de-limbed, but with a nose . . . a nose tumultuously bent . . . the Grecian angel, eyes, . . . eyes ungodly yet sparkling of divination, a mouth sweet-watered and——

Abruptly from the street below, the sound of loud voices: "We've won the war, we've won the war!"

Why always at these beatific times, why?

MARCUS *and* JULIAN *cross downstage.*

The young things who didn't have to fight are celebrating . . .

MARCUS: For a while it looked like a revolution, and now everything's turned out so well . . .

LA MONDE: Just look at them, will you?

MARCUS: It's over.

LA MONDE: Fortunately, I was too old!

MARCUS: I wonder what it was like over there?

Street sounds lessening.

LA MONDE: Good Marcus, you could say you lost it in the war.

MARCUS: Huh?

Street sounds end.

LA MONDE: One-arms shall always be in demand . . .

Pause.

MARCUS: It's time!

LA MONDE: It was nothing more than a job, was it?

MARCUS: Sir, do you always write about sad things?

LA MONDE: I am Julian La Monde. I am a poet. It's all I know.

MARCUS: But it makes you happy to touch my accident?

LA MONDE: Very!

MARCUS, *warm laughter.*

Tell me, what are you thinking?

MARCUS: It's getting dark, I have to go . . .

LA MONDE: Please don't.

MARCUS *stops.*

Good Marcus, I don't ask that you love me, that you be my gift of surrender. Only that for a whisper of time you be generous and kind in proportion to your heroic stature.

MARCUS (*shaking* LA MONDE's *hand*) : I needed the money real bad, thank you!

LA MONDE (*maintaining handshake*) : "Sir, does Joe Bremm live here!" (*Loudly laughing.*) The old trick, but such new verve!

MARCUS: He did owe me twenty bucks, Joe Bremm. He did used to live here, Mr. La Monde, no purpose lying to a man like you! (MARCUS *runs from room.*)

LA MONDE: In the fall of the year, so, so, so much, much must fall. (*Taking out handkerchief, blowing his nose loudly.*) Oh, why is it the saddest season?

13

3

The Window Across the Street

Table stage right, on which sit telephone, high pile of telegrams and letters, utensils and plates set down for eating. CANDY CANE, *blonde young woman, blanket-wrapped baby in arms, marching in circles about room. A pedometer, buttoned to her skirt, sounds as she moves.* LEROY STARR, *pencil mustache, garishly dressed, stands upstage.*

LEROY STARR: But what about my plan, my genius plot, greatest thing I ever thought up?

CANDY CANE: Leroy, please get back in the closet and close the door. Marcus'll be home any second.

> LEROY STARR *starting upstage,* CANDY CANE *crosses to stage-right window.*

LEROY STARR (*stopping*) : Candy honey, just look at you. (*Crosses to* CANDY CANE, *straightening shoulders to elevate her breasts.*) That's better, out and straight ahead! (*Rubbing* CANDY's *shoulders.*) Our America's upside down, Candy sweet, people tromp around in tears, their heads jangling with fire. Our wondrous citizens are lost and I tell you why. All the big names are dead, gone. They got nothing to look

15

up to, no new personalities, no celebrated stars. I'm using you to save our America, to raise its hope and head, my life's calling; and then you moan 'cause I won't let you ——

CANDY CANE: Leroy!

LEROY STARR: You'll tell him?

CANDY CANE: Promise!

LEROY STARR *rushes into hiding,* CANDY CANE *wandering to window.*

Junior, across the street, there he is again . . . that man, staring at us . . . (*Loudly:*) Hey Mister, why don't you leave us alone! (*Suddenly screaming out window.*) If you'd dare open your window, you'd hear me, wouldn't you?

Suddenly from street below, sounds of shouting, the din of marching feet.

Look at 'em, Junior, they're going crazy! (*Breaking into song.*)

> Junior, remember you were born from love,
> Born from love, born from love,
> And who out there can say it?
> By a Daddy dear and a Mommy warm
> Not by chance but chosen born
> And who down there can say it?

Oh, Junior, Junior, we wanted you, isn't that beautiful? For two months before we made you, I gave up preventatives, and your famous Daddy went into sacrifice, never once touched it. It was no easy matter for a tigerish man like Daddy, but I helped, watching him every second, keeping him from the john, never leaving him by himself in bed. The two of us were like foaming animals those final days, then bam, the decided time . . . and over and over 'til we could hardly walk. (*Spinning in place, sound from street fading.*) Just imagine how many of those people down there were concocted in alleys by mothers and fathers who don't even remember how it happened. Goddamn it, how lucky we are!

MARCUS *bursts running into the room.*

I was just practicing my singing on the baby!

No response, MARCUS *smiles.*

You used to talk so much, all the time, and now all you do is smile . . .

No response from MARCUS. CANDY CANE *abruptly direct, gesturing to table.*

The telegrams, the letters, they never stop. Today there's even one from Washington with a government stamp. The President, some senator? Why not open 'em and have done with it? Yes, and the phone rings on and on. A return call and the matter is dead, but oh no—and that sports writer again about the interview who only wants—— Honey, have done with these businesses and you'd be left alone like you want to . . . (*Crossing to window.*) You used to talk so much, all the time, and now all you do is smile. That guy was staring at us again.

17

MARCUS: You ought to get a curtain.

CANDY CANE: He's gone now. So much, all the time, and now all you do is smile.

MARCUS: I'll pick one up tomorrow.

CANDY CANE: I wonder what that bastard over there does when he's not spying on us.

Suddenly from street below, music, chanting people, the loud clear words of "We've won the war, we've won the war!" MARCUS *rushing to window.*

Hey, what do you say we go to bed right now, huh, forget everything and go to bed?

MARCUS: Really something, isn't it?

CANDY CANE (*checking pedometer on skirt, sound of dial turning*) : I walked three-and-a-half miles since you left.

MARCUS: The noise. Let's wait until it passes.

CANDY CANE: I still love you . . .

Marcus points to his ear, suggesting inaudibility.

Boy, do I wish you'd grab my breasts, right now!

MARCUS (*laughing, again pointing to ear*) : We'll have to wait!

CANDY CANE (*yelling*) : Today I dreamt you were back pitching again and that there were pictures of us in all the papers . . .

Street noise dying. LEROY STARR *suddenly appears upstage left, waving hand to* CANDY, *grunt of exasperation.*

MARCUS (*turning from window*) : What was that?

CANDY CANE: The war, and everyone said it would never end.

MARCUS: I heard a noise . . .

CANDY CANE: The war . . . it's over!

MARCUS: For a while it looked like a revolution . . .

CANDY CANE (*laughing*) : Come on and give Candy Cane a kiss!

MARCUS *crosses and kisses* WIFE *on forehead.*

How's your arm today?

MARCUS: Great!

CANDY CANE *suddenly slaps at* BABY.

What's wrong with you?

CANDY CANE *motionless, staring at* BABY. MARCUS *hugs* CANDY.

I promise I'll get a curtain tomorrow, first thing, and then you and Junior'll have the whole place to yourself.

CANDY CANE: I know. Please be careful or you'll hurt the baby.

MARCUS *playing with* BABY *in wife's arms,* CANDY CANE *abruptly turning head, looking up left in direction of* LEROY STARR *hiding.*

MARCUS: Let me hold him?

CANDY *gives no response.*

Candy Cane, let me hold Junior? It's been long enough, hasn't it? Why don't you let me hold him?

CANDY CANE: Hold him? Oh, no, no, no, not yet! (*Turning head back, she smiles nervously.*) No, no, he's still not used to your arm, but soon though, very, very soon . . . You know it's still too early. . . .

MARCUS: You O.K.?

CANDY CANE (*abruptly loud*): If your arm bothers you, why don't you just say so . . . have done with it, admit it! (*Pause.*) Suddenly it's gotten so quiet . . .

MARCUS: Maybe I ought to start cooking supper?

Starting to move up left, but CANDY CANE *grabs him.*

CANDY CANE: They didn't send you out caddying today, did they, and you're afraid to tell me?

MARCUS *moves away, smiling,* CANDY *in pursuit.*

You're afraid, aren't you, aren't you—that's it!

MARCUS: Nope! (*Reaching into his pocket, taking out a handful of money, giving it to her.*) For you, a surprise!

CANDY CANE (*taking money with free hand, but other hand taken up by baby. Confused, passes* JUNIOR *to* MARCUS): Here, you hold him . . . (*Counting money.*) Marcus, please hold him on your good side. Now I've lost the count . . . 25, 35, 55, 60, 65, 70 . . . Honey, there's 70 bucks here, 70 bucks!

MARCUS: There was more, but I dropped some running!

CANDY CANE: Well, where'd you get it?

MARCUS: Who cares, we got it on our own, right, Son?

CANDY CANE: Here, let me have the baby back!

MARCUS *hands* JUNIOR *back.*

He's shaking . . .

MARCUS: Now we'll be able to pay the rent . . .

CANDY CANE: I know, I know—but how'd you ever get all this?

MARCUS: Performing.

CANDY CANE: Performing?

MARCUS *shakes head "yes."*

Come on Sykowski, come on, tell me how it happened!

MARCUS: Listen, I'll tell you when I get back. (*Starting to exit.*)

CANDY CANE: Marcus, I have something to tell you.

MARCUS: Listen, the guy who gave me the money wants me to do another bit tonight, I don't know, it's to do with some commercial or something . . .

CANDY CANE: Marcus, don't leave me alone again!

MARCUS *stops, they look at each other.*

You scared Junior so much, he's peed all over my arm.

MARCUS: You'll have to go easier with me. From you I need encouragement. Listen, I gotta run!

MARCUS *bursts out of room;* LEROY STARR *appears upstage, long growl of exasperation.*

LEROY STARR: Why couldn't you lay it to him, why?

CANDY *shrugs her shoulders.*

Well listen, kid, try again tomorrow, O.K.? Kid, I know it, it's a plan of genius, get all of us where we want to go. (*Fondling baby's head.*) Got to get over your shyness, could destroy us!

Starting to exit, stopped by CANDY's *burst of laughter.*

CANDY CANE: Look, Leroy, you have pee-pee all over your hand. It shines!

LEROY STARR (*rushing back, grabbing* CANDY *by hair*): Honey Baby Doll, this is not joke time, no, no, no! Our America's grinding to crumbs, screaming for us to step forward, and all we are so far is a set of sweet tits, which is very scary, get me, so we move quick to business . . . get me?

LEROY STARR *exits.* CANDY *to table, opening dress to breastfeed son.*

CANDY CANE: Junior, your daddy last year was voted the greatest pitcher of the modern era. Now all he does is confuse everybody . . .

4
The War Is Over

TWO PEOPLE *sit across from each other at a dinner table, eating. Long silence, then* WOMAN *giggles.*

MARTHA PEABODY (*laughing on*) : Every night while you were gone, I'd always watch the news on the eleven o'clock television, and I'd hear about how many men had been killed, praying dearly you weren't one of them and then all of a sudden you're home, sitting with me . . . and all I can do is laugh—— (*Suddenly stopping, returns to eating food; long pause, again loud laughter.*) Miniver, I'm truly sorry, I am, but I don't know what's come over me . . . (*Reaching hand across table to husband.*) God bless these strange times when we can't talk to what's going on inside of us . . . (*Goes back to eating.*) Minnie, I wish you could tell me what it was like over there. (*Pause.*) You'll tell me later. (*Another outburst of laughter.*) Here I go again. . . .

MINIVER PEABODY (*mouth heartily full*) : Cooking's improved since I left . . .

MARTHA: . . . Yes . . .

Pause.

23

MINIVER: It's changed, everything has . . .

MARTHA: You haven't . . .

Pause.

Except that in the front you've lost some of your hair . . .

MINIVER: It's cut short . . .

MARTHA: You're in direct light. I can see the white of your scalp . . .

MINIVER: It'll grow back . . .

MARTHA: It must have been the awful weather over there . . .

MINIVER: In the Army you cut your hair short!

MARTHA: There are globules of sweat running down your head, I can see them.

They look at each other.

You're warm because your uniform's made of wool. (*Eating.*) You look very handsome in it. (*Pause.*) Do you think you'll ever take it off?

MINIVER: Soon . . .

MARTHA: I was faithful while you were away.

MINIVER: Yes . . .

MARTHA (*eating*): It confused me . . . (*Suddenly another outburst of laughter.*) Oh, why can't I control myself? Was it a regular thing, thinking of me while you were away?

Pause.

MINIVER: Only when I was with a woman . . .

MARTHA: Did it work?

MINIVER: Once . . .

24

MARTHA: Men are different, aren't they?

MINIVER *laughing.*

Miniver?

MINIVER: That's what I thought too . . . until I went away.

Bell from door suddenly rings; the two stare at each other.

I'm glad to be home . . .

MARTHA: You always would answer it before you left. Let's keep things the way they were . . .

MINIVER *rises and crosses stage left, disappearing; several seconds, mumbling from offstage.*

Is everything O.K. out there?

MINIVER (*unseen*) : Mister, I'm afraid I couldn't do that!

MARTHA (*rising from table*) : Minnie, what is it? (*Crossing stage left, disappearing.*) Minnie, don't you know who he is?

MINIVER *returns onstage, standing by dinner table, observing offstage.*

VOICE FROM OFFSTAGE: It's been a long time, hasn't it?

MARTHA: But you look the same.

VOICE FROM OFFSTAGE: You look even better . . .

MARTHA: You came looking for me, didn't you?

VOICE FROM OFFSTAGE: No, I was running and just happened onto your door.

MARTHA: It's wonderful to see you again!

VOICE FROM OFFSTAGE: May I come in . . .

MINIVER *(tone of exasperation)* : Martha, who *is* this guy?
MARTHA: Well, come on in . . .

MARCUS *and* MARTHA *appear.*

Place isn't much, but we're very happy. *(Laughing.)*
Thought I'd do better, didn't you? Well, go on and
tell me . . . expectations were greater.
MARCUS *(laughing warmly)* : Say, why don't you intro-
duce me to your husband?
MARTHA: Miniver, you *do* know who this is, don't you?

Exasperated, shaking his head "no," MARTHA *slapping her husband on the head.*

It's Marcus Sykowski, stupid, the guy I went to
school with, the great baseball player of Boston I'm
always telling you about.
MINIVER: You mean to say—— *(Shaking* MARCUS' *hand
vigorously.)* Marcus, finally I get a chance to see you
face to face . . . used to follow you in the papers
. . . a ballplayer you were, some ballplayer! Here,
sit down.
MARCUS *(sitting down)* : Thank you . . .
MINIVER *(excitedly)* : It is you, isn't it, I mean, who
would have ever thought the great Sykowski——?
MARCUS: I know . . .
MARTHA: I've missed you all these years, you know.
MINIVER: Kid, I read about what happened in the papers.
Was real sad . . .
MARTHA: Have you ever thought about me again in all
these years?
MINIVER: Marcus lost his arm, Martha!

MARTHA: Really?

MINIVER: Kid, go on and show her . . .

MARCUS, *with his right hand, lifts the unfilled sleeve of his raincoat.*

Hey kid, was at Fenway the night you blazed the one-hitter against the Yanks. Boy, is this exciting!

MARTHA: Does it hurt much?

MARCUS *shakes his head "no."*

Is it cauterized?

MARCUS *shakes his head "yes."*

MINIVER: I read in the paper no one knows how it happened . . . you are the great Sykowski, aren't you?

MARTHA: I read in the paper that they've made cauterizing so good that you're left with a surface as smooth and hard as a stomach. . . .

MINIVER: I read in the paper some guy up in Maine, when he heard you got your arm chopped, went to bed and burned himself to death with gasoline, and with a monkey next to him no less . . . wow, were you well-liked, huh?

MARCUS: His name was Lurtsema. He was at every game I pitched at Fenway Park.

MARTHA: Marcus, tell Miniver what was the nickname you gave me when we were in school . . .

MINIVER: I just got back from the war. (*Onto his heels, stiff-backed and proud.*)

MARCUS: There was almost a revolution while you were away, but then everything turned out O.K.

MARTHA: It was Gums, 'member, Gum-Gums Rose, 'member?

MINIVER: I was hoping they would draft you, but then when I heard about your arm, well——

MARCUS: They flunked me because of my knee.

MARTHA: Miniver, Marcus was the first man I ever slept with, you know . . .

MARCUS (*to* MINIVER): Martha forgot to tell me your name!

MINIVER: I read in the paper some girl in Hingham, Mass., killed herself the day you got chopped and then left some note no one could understand, some poetry crap, except there was something at the bottom of it 'bout "Give this to Marcus Sykowski, he's the only one who could understand . . ."

MARTHA: Newspapers are always exaggerating. I don't believe it.

MINIVER: Bet you'll miss all those people cheering now that you can't play ball any more?

MARCUS *jumps up, crossing for door, but suddenly stops.*

Martha, ask him what's the matter!

MARTHA: Marcus, what's the matter?

MARCUS (*turning from doorway, smiling*): A man in a raincoat was followin'—— A fan, nothing more. That's how I happened in here.

MARTHA: Gums Rose, go on, say what you used to call me . . . please!

MARCUS: Do you think I could have a glass of water before I go?

MARTHA, *giggling, goes for water; two men now alone.*

Isn't it absolutely amazing that of all places around here I just happened to find this one? Boy oh boy, is this a day of coincidences.

MINIVER *rises, crosses to* MARCUS.

MINIVER: Every day we were fighting, then all the way home on the ship, all we talked about was the Red Sox and how they were a cinch for the pennant next year, but now, now what's gunna happen to them, huh, now what's gunna happen?

He punches MARCUS' *armless shoulder violently, knocking him down.*

MARTHA (*returning with glass of water*) : Marcus, please understand him. He just got back and sometimes he forgets.

MARCUS (*grimacing with pain, getting off floor*) : Martha, it was nice to see you again.

MARTHA: You were my first cherished thing, and I've never forgotten . . .

MINIVER *crosses to chair and, sitting down, puts face in his hands.*

MARCUS: I wouldn't worry about it, mister, 'cause I'm still gunna pitch next spring and win your pennant too!

Exiting, MARTHA *crosses to* MINIVER, *patting his head.*

MARTHA: Come on, chicken, let me take you to bed . . .

MINIVER (*sobbing*): You're staring at my scalp again, aren't you?

MARTHA: I've been waiting so long, let's go to bed.

5

A Lost and Cherished Heart

Radio station. Sound of rock music, loud and driving, several seconds. Microphone voice from above suddenly interrupts.

MICROPHONE VOICE FROM ABOVE: We interrupt WLDD, Kinetuckmuc and Rockwater Harbor, Maine, the heart of down sounds on eleven-hundred megacycles. People, we pause to bring you words of public interest. Although the following has our station manager Captain B. D. Kilbourne's say-so, we at WLDD are in no way favoring or responsible for what you are about to hear . . .

OLD MAN appears, helped along by YOUNG MAN carrying microphone on stand. Stand is set, OLD MAN handed typed paper. YOUNG MAN turning to go, but OLD MAN grabs him firmly by neck.

OLD MAN: We pay our way, buster!

Reaching into pocket, OLD MAN flips YOUNG MAN a coin. He exits. OLD MAN reads typed paper quizzically, mumbling to self.

VOICE: Fifteen seconds, pops . . . You're sweating at the temple and under the chin, causes static . . . wipe it!

OLD MAN *wipes suggested areas with arm of lumber-jack shirt.*

Six, five, four, three, two, one. Go, pops!

OLD MAN (*into microphone, clearing throat, reads from paper. Words uneven, come in spurts*): To every one of you people within the sound of my voice which on dynamite-tonight WLDD stretches into Boston and below, I am searching the whereabouts of Marcus Sykowski, ace pitcher of the Boston Red Sox. I am Tucker Lurtsema of Kinetuckmuc, Maine, the brother of Gyles Lurtsema of whom most of you have probably read in the papers; that sadly poor, great, anti-communist, everlastingly beloved fisherman brother of mine who was confla- . . . confla- . . . con- . . . con- . . .

VOICE: CON-FLA-GRA-TED!

OLD MAN: Who burned himself with his pet monkey Marco week ago Sunday . . .

VOICE: Just what's written down, pops!

OLD MAN: Anyway, we wants you, Marcus, to come up here and attend to Gyles' funeral, Wednesday coming. Now, we know everybody sayin'——

VOICE: What's on the paper, pops, just what's written down!

OLD MAN (*yelling*): Eat a raw fish, buster! (*Throwing paper to floor, stamps on it.*) Now we know every person sayin' he burned himself 'cause of your accident with the arm, but that don't mean nothin' to us, see, Marcus . . . see, 'cause Gyles saw all your games and well . . . that says you was friends, you musta well-liked each other. So it'd be a real honor for him you could come to the services, not to mention all us Lurtsemas of Gyles' who're assembling and . . . dwelt in Maine since year after Napoleon drove our people from Poland. Also be an extra treat for Lancy Perkins' parents you make a show. See, Marcus, see, that same day we also burying Lancelot Perkins, a great little kid who drowned day 'fore Sunday last swimming beyond the break-rock where he heard the dangers and shouldna been. Now little Lancy was always feedin' Gyles' monkey peanuts and steak chips wasn't his that he stole, and so natural Lancy was fond of you as Gyles because they always read the paper together 'bout your pitchin' and anyway Gyles got all his spirit money from Lancy sellin' the programs he took back from Fenway Park after——

VOICE: To it, pops, get to it!

OLD MAN (*yelling*): Buster, how's about a suck on whale blubber! (*Back to calm, smiling.*) Besides, Lancy's the greatest Little League pitcher Kinetuckmuc ever knew. Marcus Sykowski, or a person knows him, why call him . . ., you come up here for the funeral here Wednesday, before dawn . . . which is a bit early, but it's fishin' season now and cold. Yes sir, you come up and find Gyles' relations since we got plenty of room and, goddamn it, the president of Rock-water Lumber and Nail can make it here for Polish

Feast Day of St. Mary month ago May, no reason a simple old athlete can't do like him. Sign autographs, taste our kakrinka salad, few photo shots, real fun for you, besides you must be a little lost since the arm went . . . so you need us much as we'd love to have you . . . Marcus Sykowski, as one Polack to another, you owe me an ear! Show up else I come lookin' after you. Your dad, rest his soul, musta told you 'bout our people always gettin' what they go after. See you Wednesday, Marcus Sykowski, you come on home. Thank you lots for hearin' what I was——

But rock music blares back on, cutting him off. YOUNG MAN *reappears, removing microphone.* OLD MAN, *confused and overwhelmed by shattering sound, screams:*

You ask me, all radio people bunch of shit-stinkin' cocksuckers!

6

In the Dark the Light Is Bright

Sykowski apartment. From a radio wallows music, low and warm. Darkness. Initially only voices are heard, nothing seen.

CANDY CANE (*giggling, happy*): Marcus, your fingers are cold!

> *Giggling on,* MARCUS *complimenting her with comic animal sounds.*

I can feel the calluses on your pitching grip, they're itchy! (*Uncontrollable laughter.*) Ple—ple—please . . . gotta st-o-o-op, Candy Cane's . . . getting . . . a . . . a . . . a . . . a, no, no, no . . . a (*hiccuping*) a . . . cramp, cramp!

MARCUS: Come on, I want to feel it.

CANDY CANE (*again hiccuping*): But get your hand away for a . . . no, no . . . no (*Sudden silence.*) O.K., go ahead . . . (*Suppressed low giggling.*)

MARCUS: How's my hand?

CANDY CANE: Still cold!

MARCUS (*excitedly*) : I can feel it, I can, I can!

CANDY CANE: My stomach's your favorite . . .

MARCUS: I can, I can . . . I can feel the baby, the baby!

CANDY CANE (*startled*) : What? Here, let me feel— (*Laughing.*) Oh, what a sneaky trick to pull! (*Laughing on, suddenly stopping.*) Hey, Sykowski, why aren't you laughing?

No response.

Maybe we could have one in a while, after the comeback. You could fast again, like we did with Junior. What a foaming tiger you were those final weeks and then, bam, over and over 'til——

MARCUS: Please don't nibble my ear like that!

Suddenly phone ring blares.

Let's let it ring and feel stomachs.

Sound of phone lifted from receiver.

CANDY CANE: Hello? (*Pause.*) Fine . . .

Sound of bed creaking. MARCUS *lights cigarette, bleakly illuminating room. He is out of bed, standing next to kitchen table stacked with letters. He fingers a few.*

No . . . (*Pause.*) I will, I promise, goodbye!

Phone placed back on receiver. CANDY CANE *stares at* MARCUS. *She laughs warmly.*

The letters and telegrams are growing like beanstalks. From here they're almost to your shoulder.

Soon we'll open them, and then you'll be left alone like you want!

MARCUS (*dragging on cigarette*) : Who called?

CANDY CANE: Called? Who called? Leroy, my manager. He's got me two auditions tomorrow, one for a commercial . . . isn't that good?

MARCUS: Yeah, and my arm's growing back too!

CANDY CANE: Tell me how much you care for me.

MARCUS: You'll get the commercial.

CANDY CANE: But maybe I'll get the acting part too . . .

MARCUS: You already have. (*Puts out cigarette, turns on bed lamp and gets into bed.*)

CANDY CANE: You almost got *your* commercial, didn't you?

MARCUS: The guy wasn't where he said he'd be.

CANDY CANE: Who cares! We've got the seventy bucks!

MARCUS: After we pay the rent, we'll have ten . . . (*Laughing.*) Now it's your turn. You feel my stomach . . . Come on, I'm flexing it!

CANDY CANE: Marcus, why won't you see what Mr. Walo . . . Wal . . . you know.

MARCUS: Walendale.

CANDY CANE: The president of the Red Sox, I mean, you're the star, surely he'd give you the money for a new arm, I mean, substitute limb, if only you asked him to——

MARCUS: No handouts!

CANDY CANE: Marcus, what about me and Junior?

MARCUS: I talked to Walendale while I was in the hospital. He talked to me about Conigliaro. Blind as a bat Tony was, and he made it back. (*Laughing.*)

Walendale says Red Sox players have always been notorious for their courage.

CANDY CANE: I dreamt about Mr. Walendale while you were gone tonight! Listen: you know Leroy, my manager, well . . . he had this fantastic idea of how we could get money for your arm, I mean, he mentioned it only jokingly of course, but then after we thought about it a while, why it seemed . . . I don't know, I mean, how can a famous American figure like you have to go around almost begging——

MARCUS: Candy, if you don't want to feel stomachs, I'd like to go to sleep . . .

Pause.

Your hands are warm . . .

CANDY CANE: Weren't you ticklish, even when you were a baby?

MARCUS: Ouch!

CANDY CANE: Dear, are you O.K.?

MARCUS: My stomach's still sore from the accident . . .

CANDY CANE: Would you like to talk about it?

MARCUS: No . . .

Pause.

I don't know . . .

Pause.

Maybe some day.

Suddenly a light blazes into the room.

38

CANDY CANE (*startled*) : What's that?

MARCUS: A light.

CANDY CANE: No, no, it's a flashlight . . .

MARCUS: Let's sleep . . .

CANDY CANE: I'll bet it's that bastard across the street who's always spying on me . . .

Light disappears.

MARCUS: Good night, Candy . . .

Pause.

CANDY CANE: Marcus?

MARCUS: Candy?

CANDY CANE: Would you?

MARCUS: I would love to!

CANDY CANE (*leaping on top of him, passionate assault*) : I need you, Marcus, I really need you. (*Humping up and down wildly.*) Now your hands are warmer, much warmer. (*Sensual moan.*)

MARCUS: Easy, easy, we got all night.

CANDY CANE: Oh, oh, I'll be so careful with your accident, I promise!

Again light blazes into room, this time directly into Marcus' face.

There's that light again, and I'm not even looking at it!

Abruptly MARCUS *pushes* CANDY CANE *off him, leaping from bed. Slowly he crosses to stage right window, light following him step for step. Looking out across street, he suddenly dives to floor.*

MARCUS: I'm getting dressed. I'll see you later . . .
(MARCUS *bolts from room.*)

CANDY CANE (*getting out of bed, unzipping dressing gown
to breastfeed baby*) : Junior, Junior, it's time. Junior,
wake up!

7

Answer to a Prayer

In darkness, two giggling voices, the clatter of roller skates on wood. Brief seconds, lights up. Upstage bearded MAN *at an easel, sketching in oils a* WOMAN *who sits on an orange crate posing center stage. Both persons attired in full Roller Derby outfitting: football style, full-sleeved jersey, numbered back and front, black tights, knee pads, lightly colored shorts.* MAN *in street shoes,* WOMAN *half-calf high, black boot roller skates.*

LAVERNE JONES: So I'm resting my buns on the infield bench during the women's second break, fifth period, men's third go-around, and I'm watching you loop by, watching you jockey the jammers, watching you show off, crepe-paper streamer furling your helmet, but mostly I'm watching you watch me which is, by the way, the counter to avoid being watched if you're famous and don't like attention: watch people while they watch you and you scare their asses off. Anyway, the watching you, it doesn't work; so I figure your inviting me here's got to be more than a trick for my pussy. Then you says, "Let's skate here after the game through the streets without changin' uniforms," and terrible bored with always bathing and perfuming to fool people by being sweet-scented which my manager says is one way to stay on top but there are better ones, he's Canadian . . . so I come and I'm surprised, you're legit, it's an honest-to-God art dwelling which you obviously ain't borrowing for the night since that brush looks professional, natural in your paw, yup, the feeling is surprise and it's the first time since 1963 a man's surprised old Laverne. Jasper, how I wish I could do more than just sit and smile . . . it's been so long, and I sit and smile.

JASPER TERHUNE: Turn upward, more to the light . . .

LAVERNE *does accordingly.*

Hold it there!

LAVERNE: In night light, under fluorescent tubes, so much of me must be scratched and uneven. For sure I could never be a professional. (*Pause, quiet sound of sobbing.*) Jasper, I'm skatin' around your joint now to get my feelings rearranged!

JASPER: Don't move! I want you to look like it's the half-time of a game. (*Picking up phone, dialing, whispering.*) Mrs. Sykowski, it's late but Jasper here again and get Marcus to my place, now, this minute, 'cause it's important to his whole life. Wake him if you have to and it's already morning, sure, but back to bed and God bless your patience with my calling, good night! (*Receiver replaced,* JASPER *continues to paint.*) I can't hear your sobbing now, Laverne. Please try again, slobber all you're able. It adds a lot to the canvas.

SHE *giggles,* HE *giggles, loud burst of laughter, then abrupt silence.*

Every week *Rolling Skate* magazine calls you the greatest female player the game has ever had . . .

LAVERNE: Last week *Big Jam* said you and Niemiah Slick were the hottest rookie jammers since Ronnie Ray Cole in '56 and they haven't even caught the surprise of your painting yet!

JASPER: *Rolling Skate* says that you and Ronnie Ray off nights get it down so much, the first game back you can hardly skate. Three cheers for Ronnie Ray!

LAVERNE: And *Big Jam* keeps suggesting with pictures that I'm lesbo. Who's to know? . . .

JASPER: Everybody knows all they got are photographic blast-ups falsified by overlay . . .

LAVERNE: *Rolling Skate* says I dye my hair, that at that it's not my own. They say I wear contact lenses driving, have secret a blue-eyed son and support relatives up and down the coast. Jasper, why can't they mention once I wear falsies every game against the Cleveland Hornets to upset Joanie James . . . which explains for us always winning?

JASPER: Unlace your skates a little, Laverne. The ankles and feet are finished and I've moved to the middle.

LAVERNE: Jasper, could I visit you regularly after games, would that be fun for you?

JASPER: Of course, I owe it. That's why I'm catching on so quick, watching you skate every night! You were the best you've ever been tonight.

LAVERNE: Twice before you came to skating I was better.

43

Twice I scored fourteen in the Garden, in championships against Joanie James, and seventeen once in an exhibition in Back Bay Rollerama.

MARCUS *suddenly appears downstage, half rushing into room.*

MARCUS: I never figured you for a beard!

JASPER: I've turned to painting.

MARCUS: It hides your acne marks.

JASPER: I never thought of that.

MARCUS: You and the Hemingway fella, it makes me laugh!

JASPER: I'm skating Roller Derby. I'm very popular with the fans!

MARCUS: You look great in a uniform!

JASPER: Friends keep saying I've finally located myself . . . It's been years, but I had a fantastic sense you'd come.

MARCUS: My wife wonders why you keep calling.

JASPER: Roller Derby pays nicely and I'm putting together good and solid savings. Enough so come next fall I quit and though you may not believe it, but I've got visions of medical school, delicate surgery, finally put my dexterity to advantage. (*Pause.*) Hey, buddy, who beyond us ever remembers I was a better pitcher in high school and Legion both, more wins, strikeouts, lower earned-run average? Hey, buddy, will they mention it even once when your life story comes out?

MARCUS: Who could forget?

JASPER: I have no reason to be angry!

MARCUS: We went our own ways . . .

JASPER: But still you're getting more attention in the papers and magazines than even the war! . . . Which is over now, isn't it?

MARCUS (*opening arms wide*): Jasper, come and give your old bud a hug!

JASPER *crosses, accepting embrace.*

JASPER: Buddy, will they mention me being a better pitcher at the start even once when your life story comes out?

MARCUS *withdraws, stepping back, two men stare.*

Poor bastard, how could you let it happen? You were all the way to the top!

MARCUS: I ran into Gums Rose the other day . . .

JASPER: It's hard to believe, isn't it?

MARCUS: You really had a way of giving people expressive names! (*Reacting to* LAVERNE *seated upstage.*) Still got an eye for the good looking ladies, don't you!

LAVERNE (*rushing to* MARCUS): I'm Laverne Jones.

JASPER: Marcus, she's my newest friend.

LAVERNE: I don't read newspapers, they never cover skating, so I don't even know who you are. But I like you more than anyone I've met in my life!

JASPER: Marcus was the greatest pitcher in baseball before his accident, Laverne . . .

LAVERNE: How nice!

JASPER: Marcus, I have a surprise for you, an answer to all your prayers. Laverne herself doesn't even know, hasn't heard, but I have been empowered by the

45

commissioner of Roller Derby to offer you twenty-five thousand to sign with the Boston Derby Bombers, plus a gate per cent of all home games. That's why I've been calling so much.

LAVERNE: But twenty-five thousand is double more than I get, Jasper! And who's to know if a one-arm has the balance to stay up on skates, not to mention all the jockeying in the jams. It sounds to me like there's been some mistake made . . .

JASPER: A mistake, Laverne, a mistake? He's the great Sykowski! Why, he could pack our Rollergarden five times a day just letting people watch him brush and comb himself . . .

MARCUS *laughing loudly.*

See that smile, Laverne, those teeth perfectly straight, most valuable pieces of property in the whole Northeast!

MARCUS *laughing.*

There's been no mistake, Laverne. Our league signs the great Sykowski and Roller Derby can finally go big time!

LAVERNE: Roller Derby is big time, Jasper. *Rolling Skate* says often we're the biggest thing in Boston.

JASPER: So you'll take the offer, right, buddy? It's no secret you need the money . . .

MARCUS *laughing on.*

LAVERNE: Jasper, *Rolling Skate* reported last January me

and Ronnie Ray Cole were bigger in most sections of Boston than even baked beans or the President Nixon comics, so why another player? Oh, I'm sure there's been a great mistake made here!

MARCUS: Ronnie Ray Cole? Derby Bombers? Listen, I gotta get out of here before I piss on the floor!

JASPER: But skating in the Derby you'd stop humiliating yourself day after day like I keep reading about everywhere . . . Week after week of what the writers say about your guts gone weak, questioning your behavior, your sanity, oh, take the bonus, learn to skate, be reputable. Think of your family, the future. Stop all this weirdo-hero shit that's nauseating half the country's guts. Buddy, we don't need heroes these days, we need winners, you get me, the stomachs are screaming for win, win, win! The fans'd go bugshit seeing you and me skating the oval side by side . . . so whataya say?

MARCUS: Sweet pal, keep up the good work, and first time the Red Sox come north after spring training I'll stop in again.

JASPER: You can't pitch again and you know it!

MARCUS: Nice meeting you, Laverne. Continued success to you and Ronnie Ray and the Bombers. (*Turning,* MARCUS *stands to exit.*)

LAVERNE: Mister, I'm coming with you.

MARCUS: Real way with women, right, Jasper?

Suddenly the explosive ring of a gun blast, reverberating, pings of ricochet, flying glass. THREE *hit ground. Long pause, then* MARCUS *laughs.*

47

Pisser, ain't it? (*Racing offstage.*) See you folks next spring!

Several seconds and MAN IN RAINCOAT *appears next to easel, high-beam spotlight in hand.*

MAN IN RAINCOAT: Hey, you!

JASPER: Me?

MAN (*doing sudden double-take at canvas*) : Did you do that?

JASPER *nods "yes."*

Have you studied life drawing and anatomy?

JASPER *nods "yes."*

And looked into shadow-shaping and composition?

JASPER *nods "yes."*

And been extra attentive to color and the accidental-ness of the world around you?

JASPER *shrugs shoulders quizzically.*

Well, that's the problem, Junior. (*Spotlight switched on, rushes after departed* MARCUS.)

JASPER: Do you think we should call the cops?

LAVERNE: Bastard! If he hadn't come along, your friend would have taken me with him.

8
A Deal Like a Steak

Sykowski apartment. MARCUS *rushes into room, crosses stage right to kitchen table, sits. Immediately voices are heard offstage, drawing near. Man,* LEROY STARR, *and woman,* PEPPER WEITZ, *appear. They see* MARCUS.

PEPPER WEITZ: That's him . . .

LEROY STARR: That's him.

PEPPER WEITZ: The eyes are just like the cover of *Time* magazine made them the last time.

LEROY STARR: He doesn't look big as I figured . . .

PEPPER WEITZ: *Time* made his hair darker, but his cheeks are less red. Something's up!

   Pause.

LEROY STARR: Lady, are you sure it's him?

PEPPER WEITZ: At this distance, even a good person could be fooled. Let's move in!

   TWO *move closer.*

LEROY STARR: Well?

PEPPER WEITZ: It's him!

LEROY STARR: How can you be certain?

PEPPER WEITZ: He's missing an arm!

LEROY STARR: We could have checked for the stump from the start.

TWO *turn and rush from room.*

PEPPER WEITZ: Miss, we know it's him!
LEROY STARR: Candy baby, he's already here!

TWO *reappear huddling behind* CANDY CANE *with baby. She checks pedometer buttoned to skirt.*

CANDY CANE: Five miles, Junior, and it's still not afternoon.

CANDY CANE *hands baby to* PEPPER WEITZ *and starts across room.*

MARCUS (*blurting out*): I took in an all-night movie and then I counted street lights till the sun came on . . . and after that to the golf club which I went straight to, first one there as always, only it was light action so they couldn't send me out today.
CANDY CANE: You didn't get any sleep, did you?
MARCUS: The Fatman promised tomorrow for sure he could send me out.
CANDY CANE: But you know you can handle only bags that are nice and light . . .
MARCUS: You look extra sweet and tasty. I should have hung around last night. Tonight I promise we'll get to it, tonight!
CANDY CANE: . . . only ones that are nice and light and nowadays they make them all so heavy. Face it, you're not fit for the job, you're unable, you shouldn't even be there!

MARCUS: I forgot to pick up the curtains too . . . Last night, every time the movie got stupid or sloppy, I'd whisper over and over to myself, "Curtains, curtains, don't forget the curtains before you go back home . . . else the man'll keep staring!" I forgot. (*Laughing*.) I'm really something, aren't I?

CANDY CANE: Did you notice all the letters and telegrams gone? (*Pointing to kitchen table*.) I dumped them in the furnace!

MARCUS: Listen, it would have taken a dozen secretaries to answer them all. (*Gesturing* CANDY *close, whispering*.) I'm giving serious thought to ripping down the baseball card picture of me from the mailbox, so finally we'll be left alone like we want.

CANDY CANE: Marcus, Junior's going away for a while.

MARCUS: What's up? (*Joking*.) Can't sonny get used to his poor dad's stump, does the green pus bother his tummy?

CANDY CANE: He's going away for a while with Miss Weitz over there!

PEPPER WEITZ: Don't be fooled by my complexion. I have a very effective way with kids.

CANDY CANE: You're all wet, you're sweating.

MARCUS: I've been running.

CANDY CANE: Would you like to change your shirt?

MARCUS: You know how much you love my smell.

CANDY CANE (*grabbing* MARCUS *by arm, pulling him from chair to feet*) : Mr. Starr, he's the man over there, my manager?

LEROY STARR: Son, you're a legend in your own time, you and the Kennedys . . .

CANDY CANE: Marcus, he's the man I'm always telling you about.

LEROY STARR: You're the dream of every boy in America. As we say in the business, the possibilities are mind-boggling!

PEPPER WEITZ: Is Junior on a normal feeding schedule? It's important to figuring my charges.

LEROY STARR: Candy baby, I'll take over.

Taking MARCUS *by the shoulder.*

Name's Starr, my boy, Leroy Starr, finest handler of talent in the east and, like you, a giant, a biggie in my field. Starr says a person don't work and they don't peddle even Bibles or colored glass, get my point! Anyway, wife's a real find, my boy, strong "super-starlet" possibilities, plus she can act a bit. So tell you what I'm going to do: got a younger brother, Harpo by name, fine boy, in TV, WNTZ, going places, runs the whole thing. To our good fortune, Harpo's into me for a big favor, so some weekday night, into an editorial spot, we slam The Candy Cane, a whole three minutes, eyes filled with tears into that spot she goes, tears, pain, upset, the whole works. Now, no one knows she's an actress pretending, so when she gives this whole wandango about your Junior having been kidnapped, snatched from you, everyone bites, full-boat, Sykowski's a known name, star power, that touch of the legend . . . (*laughing wildly*) 'cept your little dumpling hasn't been kidnapped, not at all, because he'll be in hiding, secret, with Miss Weitz over there who the agency tells us is very experienced with caring for children.

CANDY CANE: She does come highly recommended . . .

LEROY STARR: Being a bright boy, sure you get the full potentialities of my genius plot already, read me? People call the station like crazy, great coverage in the papers, the full boat, and bam, The Candy Cane's star power, anything we want: movies, nightclubs, commercials, plays! (*Placing hands on* MARCUS' *shoulders.*) You were real hot for a while there, you can understand . . .

MARCUS: Listen, I'll be again, soon as I get my chrome piece!

LEROY STARR: It's ugly, rotten and smells, but face it, boy, you're busted and broke!

MARCUS: It's a substitute limb, operates on nerve impulses, the newest thing, came out just last year and plated in chrome. . . .

LEROY STARR: So you buy a dozen . . . just in case the chrome peels! That ain't enough, Starr'll buy the company makes the things and we'll distribute a Marcus Sykowski autograph model, and the clever suburb kids'll gobble 'em for Christmas so they can scrape the guts out and use 'em for whiffle-ball bats. Anything you want, son, anything and the Starr'll score it. Why, the whole of America's at stake and the woods are too dry not to burn, get me?

MARCUS: Candy, I can't keep it a secret any more, it must be told (*pointing firmly at* LEROY STARR) : this is the man who chopped my poor arm, this is the wicked monster!

Long pause, PEOPLE *aghast,* MARCUS *then into howling laughter.*

LEROY STARR: Son, if you were all in one piece, I'd rip your balls out of the bags and along with your root dump 'em in a fishbowl in my office for showing difficult clients. (*Now Leroy Starr into howling laughter.*) Some pair of a comedy team we'd make, huh?

CANDY CANE: Marcus, I want you to kiss Junior goodbye.

MARCUS (*kissing son*) : Son, your mother's doing all she can. Be proud of her. (*To* PEPPER WEITZ:) I'll bet you have a nice way with children.

CANDY CANE: It's her job, and she does good work.

MARCUS (*shaking* LEROY STARR's *hand*) : Sounds like a very effective plan. I appreciate your interest, sir, and thank you. Candy, I'm going to Maine after all. (*Rushing off.*) Take care of things!

LEROY STARR *grunts and yelps sounds of success, picks up* CANDY CANE, *spinning her around, then letting her down.*

CANDY CANE: I don't think he's coming back, do you?

PEPPER WEITZ: Mrs. Sykowski, my charges start today, so I'd be happy to take the kid right now if you wish.

CANDY CANE: Bring him over here, would you please, I'd like to keep him 'til suppertime.

PEPPER WEITZ *starts to cross, but* LEROY STARR *stops her.*

LEROY STARR: Candy honey, that's a little dangerous,

don't you think, ruin our plan before it even gets cooking? (*Short pause.*) It's better in every way we take Junior now, right, Miss Weitz?

PEPPER WEITZ: You're the boss, Mr. Starr.

LEROY STARR (*pushing at* PEPPER WEITZ, *baby in hand, exiting and yelling back*) : My plan'll work, it's easy as a steak!

Brief pause and TUCKER LURTSEMA *bursts panting into the room.*

TUCKER LURTSEMA: Out of hiding, Polack, I warned you! (*Notices* CANDY CANE, *sudden politeness.*) Miss, happen you to know the goings of the great Sykowski?

CANDY CANE: Maine.

Laughing, jumping, TUCKER LURTSEMA *runs from room.* CANDY CANE *crosses to window, looking out.*

Why don't you open the window, son of a bitch, and say something!

9

In the State of Maine

Graveyard. Stage in darkness. Against backstage wall, photographs are projected:

1. Graveyard—casket being lowered into ground. Crowd of people gathered, Marcus at center, hand resting on young boy's head. Next to him, Tucker Lurtsema widely smiling. To the side, newsmen with cameras snapping flash pictures.

2. Burial—dirt being shoveled into grave. Marcus, surrounded by children, signing autographs. Next to him, Tucker Lurtsema offering food and drink. To the side newsmen with cameras snapping flash pictures.

3. Prayer—Marcus, on his knees before filled grave, head turned, look of disbelief, as it is now Tucker Lurtsema to the side with camera snapping pictures.

Next MARCUS *in person appears . . . lighted by the flashbulb bursts of unseen cameras.*

MARCUS (*over grave*): For sure you're better off in one way, getting rid of that brother of yours! (*Pause.*) Listen Gyles, you and me, we gotta get something straight. I didn't know you. I wasn't a buddy, no pal. We met once. For five minutes outside Fenway Park, we met once. It was May a year ago, remember, and I had thrown my great no-hitter against the Tigers of Detroit. I hardly looked at you, my mind was somewhere else . . . (*Sudden burst of laughter.*) The fact is, Gyles, I was throwing so good that final inning, Fenway quiet as a tomb, and all I could think about was this lady in a box seat behind third base with this luscious set of grapefruits and how goddamned funny it would be stepping from the mound and laying a change of pace between her fruits, like a feather. If you felt you saw something else about me that day, you must have been dreaming, you and that goddamn monkey! And get this too! I only came here because there was nothing else. I used you and you're dead. What need is there for apologies? (*Pause.*) I read the Boston papers all the way. They want to know what's going to happen to me, Gyles, what's going to happen to my wind-up, my kick, my great balance. They say, "Why doesn't he take help from the Red Sox, for what reason did he refuse the insurance aid, what about the wife and child?" They say, the papers, they think I should say to the police how my arm was chopped, that as a great and known figure of America I owe it, a duty. But who are they to ask favors! Fortunate for sportswriters that bullshit doesn't smell. (*Pause.*) I am a pitcher. Pitching is my job. I have lost an arm, but I will *earn* it back. I have science on my side. Gyles, I'm no college man. I never got a degree. I am no thinker, no man whose job it is to lead or be understood. I am a pitcher. I stand on the mound. I hold the ball, smile, get the feel I'm ready. I rear, I fire, and that ball goes exactly where I tell it 'cause I tell it to, 'cause it was me who threw it, the great Sykowski. What else must they know? Have they never heard of the Southern League's great Grover Pepperidge? One hundred and seventy-seven games, for Chrissakes! (*Gesturing madly.*) One strike, two strikes, three strikes, four, five, six, seven, eight, nine . . . the whole side, 'cause when you're pouring rhythm sweet, when you got it, really got it, they can't see it, they can't smell it, they can't touch it, they can't even believe it . . . It's yours, all yours . . . it's magic! (*Pounding ground before grave.*) Don't they know how bad we need men of . . . mystery, honorable mystery, persons of the proper secret, and not those with it wished and pushed upon them? (*Reaching to touch shoulder socket inside coat.*) Gyles, if you could talk, you would tell me of your own wonderful mystery, wouldn't you? (*Withdrawing hand from inside coat, smelling it, inspecting fingers.*) Look, now it's begun to drain. It's all over my coat! (*Sudden energy.*) But the doctor said when it began to drain, that would mean—— Oh Gyles, you pisser, you beautiful pisser, it's good, it's healing properly. This means for sure I'm gunna pitch again! (*Arm spread wide, laughter filling his body.*)

10

People Who Came in the Night

Sykowski apartment. Upstage hangs, tacked to wall, a red curtain. Downstage left, MARCUS *on the floor in blanket, sleeping. Scattered about him on floor several balls of cotton covered with blood. Offstage left, the vague murmur of voices.* CANDY CANE *appears, followed by* TWO BURLY MEN *pushing a large, rectangular, sheet-covered box on wheels. In silence they move wheeled box center stage; in whispers, conferring with men,* CANDY CANE *hands them money.* MEN *start to exit,* CANDY CANE *tapping* ONE *on shoulder.* SECOND MAN *hands her revolver which she hides in dress pocket. Crossing downstage, she shakes husband from sleep.* MARCUS *wakes, rubs eyes and head, still half-asleep, sits up.*

MARCUS: I slept here. I didn't want to stain the sheets. I hitch-hiked home. It was a nice ride. They didn't recognize me. A young woman with a baby. She never stopped laughing! Something wonderful happened in Maine. Give me a second to wake up and I'll tell you *all* about it.

CANDY CANE, *no response.*

I was able to put my confusion into words in Maine, I found a strength for going on in Maine. Kinetuckmuc is cold but nice this time of year . . . It was good for me to go. I feel very proud.

Pause.

Now it's you who smiles and never talks.

CANDY CANE *gently placing husband's head against pelvic-stomach area. She is standing up.*

I can hear him crawling around in there.

They both laugh.

Oh, the young woman you would have loved with the baby. She never stopped laughing.

Pause.

Did that lady take Junior?

CANDY CANE: Leroy says everything's going perfectly. He says I'll be on TV Thursday.

MARCUS: I have a feeling we're going to make it after all.

CANDY *suddenly casts look at bloodied cotton on floor;* MARCUS *responding.*

That means it's healing properly. Dr. Smith said it would be the sign . . . when it came. Maybe we could visit Junior today? Doesn't it sound like a great idea?

CANDY CANE: Leroy says it would be too dangerous. He says it could ruin our plan . . .

Pause.

MARCUS: Now it's you, isn't it, who smiles and never talks? I'd like to tell you about the funeral . . . See, for a while there things got unsure, but going——

CANDY CANE: Marcus, the curtain is beautiful.

MARCUS: Then you've noticed it!

Starting to look around at curtain, CANDY CANE *grabs his head.*

CANDY CANE: Don't move. Stay where you are! (*Singing.*)

> We have come upon a curtain, a curtain,
>   a curtain,
> We have come upon a curtain, and Bad Eyes
>   can't look in again.

(*Humming song.*)

MARCUS: I'm real happy you like it . . .

CANDY CANE: It's beautiful! (*Continues humming.*)

MARCUS: Now the man across the street won't bother you any more.

CANDY CANE: Unless he finds another way. Oh, you're so good to me. How did I ever find something so beautiful?

MARCUS: Gyles' brother's named Tucker, Tucker Lurtsema? Well, he gave it to me as a present for coming to the funeral!

Suddenly stepping back, CANDY CANE *slaps her husband's face hard.*

63

CANDY CANE: I wish I could believe you!

MARCUS: Baby, is it the color of the curtain, is that what it is? So we throw it out and get another. Come on and give me another hug, please?

CANDY CANE: Not true the man gave it, no, no, no! Was it the hitch-hike lady, who was it?

MARCUS: As a present he gave it, yes he did, a present, as a gift of thanks. The Lurtsemas are generous people!

CANDY CANE: And about the man who picked you up for commercials in October?

MARCUS: He made a fool of me. He wasn't where he said he'd be.

CANDY CANE (*again violently slapping husband's face*): Not true!

MARCUS: But it was so dark and——

CANDY CANE (*cutting him off*): And about the seventy dollars he gave you?

MARCUS: He really gave me a hundred, but I dropped some running, remember, the day the war ended, it was very confusing!

Again CANDY CANE *slaps* MARCUS. *Staring at her, he suddenly falls at wife's feet.*

Yes, yes, I was lying, fibbing, sneaking. But I had to. With Gyles in Maine, I saw I must go on just as I started out, keep up—— It can't be talked about in words, explained by saying . . . (*grabbing wife behind legs*). No words, just your "yes" that you'll stick to me!

Burying head in WIFE *who herself slowly takes gun*

64

from pocket and begins, in tired anguish, to let revolver barrel droop toward kneeling HUSBAND.

Will you say "yes" and just stick? You I need!

CANDY CANE *(abruptly hiding gun)* : Marcus, I'll stick, I'll say "yes!"

MARCUS *(sudden laughter)* : On the way home in the car, there was that smell of you, the perfume you always——

CANDY CANE: People came in the night, Marcus. Toward dark last night a woman knocked on our door. She said she'd been looking for you for days. Said suddenly her husband had re-enlisted for the Army, and that you'd know where to reach her. An hour later, maybe it was two or three, a man knocked on our door. He smelled of perfume, was wearing too much. He said something about a book of poems he was dedicating to you, something about "Leonard" . . . "Leonard and the Velvet Fork." He said——

MARCUS *(quietly laughing)* : Candy, I got a hard-on in that car with the lady hitch-hiking . . . but then, then when I turned to look, there was the smell of you all over, back seat and front, the rose scent odor we joke about . . . I knew then I could count on you.

CANDY CANE: Toward midnight, just a while ago, it was beginning to rain. Another man knocked on our door. He was wearing a raincoat, except he didn't talk, wouldn't. He took off his hat, water sprayed, he stared. Finally he said, "Tell your husband we'll have to see him soon. Time's run out."

MARCUS (*laughing on, falling back on his heels*) : Candy, you're beautiful, just like a present. When I thought all I had was Gyles and now it's you too . . . Damn, opening day against the Yanks I dedicate to you, now, and it's gunna be something!

CANDY CANE (*taking husband by shirt collar*) : But what about the people who came in the night, Marcus, what about them?

MARCUS: Come on, who cares, nothing to worry about! Candy, I hardly know them!

Now, harder than ever, CANDY CANE *bashes* MARCUS' *face. Turning, crosses quickly to covered box, pulling off sheet and screams into box.*

CANDY CANE: O.K., everybody up! (*Intently whispering.*) Got the gun back again. No tricks or I'll blow your skulls out, hear me?

From inside box, JULIAN LA MONDE, MARTHA PEA-BODY, *and* MAN IN RAINCOAT *pop up, mouths gagged, hands tied behind their backs;* CANDY CANE *takes Magic Marker pen from pocket and numbers faces of victims in large scrawl, numbers 1, 2 and 3.*

MARCUS: Sure look funny, don't they? How'd you ever manage it? Must have had help, right?

CANDY CANE (*yelling*) : O.K., everybody down!

THREE PEOPLE *slowly descend, disappear, box covered again with sheet.*

MARCUS: Baby, we've got to let the guy in the raincoat go. It could give us trouble, terrible trou——

CANDY CANE: Can you understand why I've done this, gone so far, can you?

MARCUS: Sure, sure, but first we let the raincoat guy go. (*Moving toward box.*) See, he's been leaving me be lately, on my own, but this could——

CANDY CANE: Marcus Sykowski, I could reach down through your shoulder socket and squeeze your heart till it pops. I'm about to whore, parade, and lie before the TV for you, I sit without my baby in this place with my legs lifted under my bottom 'cause of bugs and roaches, and that for you too, but——

MARCUS: But you're sticking through, staying on! Like you promised. That's good, that's all that matters, right, love?

CANDY CANE (*laughing lightly*): Your shirt and crotch are smeared in sweat stain. I can feel it up my nose. You're putting poison in the air. And now you've splattered blood all over the floor. (*Short pause.*) All I want right now is for you to take a shower, O.K.?

MARCUS: But the guy in the raincoat could ruin all——

CANDY CANE: No! Now . . . Go! (*Nervously hand to pocket, hiding revolver.*) Before I . . . Go, I said, go!

CANDY CANE *pointing stage left,* MARCUS *slowly exits toward shower.* CANDY *alone, plays with cotton blood ball on floor. Water in shower heard.*

MARCUS (*from offstage, loudly through sound of shower*): You were right! I didn't realize how dirty I'd gotten . . . (*Laughter.*) Candy love, now you know just how it feels, right? Beautiful thing, isn't it?

CANDY CANE: Marcus, what is it now?

MARCUS: Your great secret, stupid, getting the strangers in the box? Must have been some trick, capturing those strangers like you did! But that's all I mention. Know how everyone deserves their special secret . . . Listen, we'll decide what to do with them, then hop right into bed.

CANDY CANE (*crossing to box, revolver from pocket, aimed within*) : I'd let one of you go right now if you'd tell me how to help my husband.

Singing from shower.

11
Strike at the Country Club

Loud laughter, lights slowly up. As in Scene 1, long wooden bench backstage. As before, loudspeaker socketed to the proscenium frame. Occupying bench, LAVERNE JONES, *Roller Derby lady from Scene 7, center of attention, now in skirt but with Roller Derby jersey top still same. Next to her and seated,* MARCUS. *Surrounding them, six caddies laughing loudly at story* LAVERNE JONES *in process of telling. Laughter heightening, several men in excitement playfully pushing at each other.*

DELORENZO (*raising hands to quiet group*) : O.K., boys, O.K., O.K.! Let's let the nice lady finish her story.

Sudden silence, PEOPLE *darting glances at one another.*

Miss Jones, go on and finish.

LAVERNE JONES: Normally I'm not at all this free with men . . . (*Grabbing firm hold of* MARCUS.) Marcus, you're so like my Ronnie Ray in the early days, so the same with those dreamy eyes like they're looking just above the tops of everything. When you ran from Jasper's the other night, I knew I had to follow after till I found you, caught up with you no matter——

STANLEY KUCKTA (*interrupting, great slowness of speech, as if each word were a sentence by itself*): Miss Laverne, don't you want to tell us like you promised the part where you and Ronnie Ray first met and became pals?

Pause.

It seems to me you should want to tell us like you promised the part where you and Ronnie Ray first met and became pals?

Pause.

You do want to tell us . . . I think——

Pause.

Make me know what I think, Miss Laverne.

LAVERNE: I had been in Roller Derby two years when my Ronnie Ray was hired to drive the truck that carried the derby track, portable it was, that we skated on then and lugged from town to town. They had told my Ronnie Ray to make up for the small pay that they would let him skate the final games of the Western tour as first-sub jammer. It was a promise they said, but never kept. My Ronnie Ray was upset and in time started to wander secretly away for hours. One day we stopped in Walkerville, on Lake Erie above Cleveland and as was regular Ronnie Ray went off, but this time didn't come back for going on to the arena to set down the track. I looked for hours and then he was there. I found my Ronnie in the hardware store in Walkerville, back by the nails of tanium and zinc, where no one goes because they fear the chemical fumes tanium most of all gives off. I caught him there pounding a five-inch stud of zinc into his stomach. With a hacksaw he'd ripped from the wall, he'd already ravaged his wrists. To hold the bleeding we left the nail where it was, I kept his hands away and we ran through the crowded store. I was not a well woman at the time. On the way to the hospital, I fell in love with the color and thickness of Ronnie Ray's blood that splattered my shirt and slid across the vinyl seat under both our legs. It took him three months and a week to get better, and so for the season I left Roller Derby and took a job as a waitress across from the ward where they had my man strapped and visited him every day. One Sunday they let him out. We took a week hiding away to get used to the awful scars and then onto Boston, this city, we came and lived so feebly, so cheaply, but with hope made love before breakfast each day—with roaches and bugs upon us every time a chunk of plaster pulled from the wall. By day I worked with cripples for money and after supper to the Roller-ama where Ronnie Ray learned to outskate me so quick I knew he was born to the roller legend he's become. Oh, those dreamy eyes like they're above the tops of everything, the great Marcus and my Ronnie Ray so the same . . .

MARCUS: Is that the end?

LAVERNE *nods "yes."*

Then squeeze your cheeks and get the hell out of here!

LAVERNE: I don't understand . . .

MARCUS: Honey, what you need is . . . is a ream job and a new set of falsies . . . (*Pinching her chest.*) Now get up and move!!!

LAVERNE (*spits in* MARCUS' *face*) : Sonny boy, not one of my sons ever even touches a goddamned baseball, hear me?

LAVERNE *exits.* MARCUS *looks at* MEN *around him, slaps hand to thigh, laughing loudly.*

MARCUS: Honey, what you need is a ream job and a new set of falsies . . .

Pause.

Boys, did you see her face when I said that!

Pause.

Boys, some imagination, haven't I?

Feeble chorus of "yeahs."

KUCKTA (*Mongoloid slowness*) : Marcus?

O'CONNOR: Speak up, Stanley, no one'll hurt you!

KUCKTA: Marcus, why don't you go after her? It seems to me she wants you to go after her . . . and explain.

Pause.

Doesn't she want you to go after her, or am I not seeing she doesn't want you to go after her?

Pause.

72

She does want you to go after her . . . and explain
. . . I think. . . .

O'CONNOR (*slapping* KUCKTA *hard on the head*) : What's
the matter with you, stupid, the guy's upset by
something!

MARCUS: O'Connor, leave Stanley alone . . .

DELORENZO: Kid, he's got to learn to ask good questions.

DILLINGER: And we're his teacher!

KUCKTA: But, O'Connor, you're married and that doesn't
stop you from going after ladies who want you to go
after them!

O'CONNOR: Dummy, what are you babbling about?

KUCKTA: Marcus can't be that different from you, us
either, O'Connor . . .

Pause.

Many times he's said he's happy here 'cause he's just
like the rest of us. O'Connor, I think you can't help
it ladies want you to go after them.

KOLKOWSKI (*laughing loudly*) : Sing on, idiot boy, you're
the most!

O'CONNOR: Shut up, pigface, 'fore I——

MARCUS: She's not like you guys. She couldn't see my
comedy. You laugh. But them, them all I do is
confuse . . . I was trying to use a reverse method,
but she couldn't feel my humor, figure it out!

Pause.

I don't know.

KUCKTA: I do, but I won't bring it out.

O'CONNOR: Aw, shut it off, will ya!

KOLKOWSKI: Marcus, I don't understand what——

O'CONNOR: Listen, he was just saying something to keep Stanley happy. We know he wouldn't go after no pig like that; you heard what he told her!

MARCUS (*laughing to himself*) : Maybe it's really me who needs the ream job. . . .

DELORENZO (*jumping up, laughing*) : Hey kid, why's it always me the only one who can understand you, huh? Boys, let's hear how bad we want to hear the kid laugh again?

Chorus of "yeahs."

LOUDSPEAKER (*blurting suddenly*) : Boys, this is your happy fatman speaking. Now listen, either you cut out this sit-down-strike crap or I send my muscle man Myles back. O.K. Kolkowski . . . on 88 and 17.

DELORENZO: Not here! Now let's hear when was the last time Marcus was clean, huh . . . so clean and spruced up?

KOLKOWSKI: Were worried there for a spell you were going to smell us out 'cause of your unbathing . . . ain't that right, boys!

Chorus of "yeahs."

KUCKTA: JoJo's right, Marcus.

LOUDSPEAKER: Dillinger . . . on 39 and 73.

DELORENZO: Not here!

SHATTUCK: Come on and tell a baseball story that's funny, Marcus.

KUCKTA: They want you to laugh, Marcus Sykowski.

KOLKOWSKI: Yeah, kid, one of those stories you always used to tell!

DELORENZO: Boys, what do you say we give him a little peace.

LOUDSPEAKER: Oh, I'm getting bugged. O.K. now, O'Connor on 39 and 73!

O'CONNOR *starting to rise, but* DELORENZO *shoves him back to bench.*

DELORENZO: He's not here yet!

O'CONNOR: JoJo, you tell me why I shouldn't go out, after the way he made a fool of me, huh?

LOUDSPEAKER: We know he's there. Now let's move it!

O'CONNOR: He's not here yet!

MARCUS: JoJo, you guys shouldn't refuse to go out because of me . . .

DELORENZO: Forget it.

KOLKOWSKI: We're all behind you, kid, so don't worry about it, O.K.! Ain't that right, boys?

Chorus of "yeahs."

LOUDSPEAKER: Let's go, O'Connor, 39 and 73! People are waiting.

O'CONNOR: But he's not here, sir. He's at his mother's having brunch!

MEN *laugh uproariously, then sudden pause of silence.*

SHATTUCK: We didn't understand you for a while, kid, but now we're happy to have you back.

DELORENZO: Me and my Momma are finally getting on, now that she knows I'm friends to you. I appreciated that.

DILLINGER: Yeah, and who ever thought guys like us get a chance to work next to a national celebrity?

Voices of agreement.

DELORENZO: Things must be pretty good at home, huh, kid?

MARCUS: Candy's been wonderful.

KUCKTA: I remember when you said that last.

LOUDSPEAKER: Kuckta on 39 and 73!

DELORENZO: Not here!

KUCKTA: JoJo, I have to go out. My mother needs the money for her medicine.

MARCUS: Go on, Stanley, I understand . . .

DELORENZO: Get up, Stanley, and we snap your back!

KOLKOWSKI: We all agreed?

Chorus of "yeahs."

LOUDSPEAKER: Let's go, Kuckta, 'fore I send Myles back there and whip your ass!

O'CONNOR: He's home with his mommy, petting her sick hand.

LOUDSPEAKER: Kuckta, 39 and 73, they're waiting. Stanley, you got ten seconds or I send Myles . . .

KUCKTA (*jumping up*): My mother's very sick. I've got to have the money!

DELORENZO: Stanley, sit down!

MARCUS: Let him go, will ya, his moth——

DELORENZO: Stanley, down!

KUCKTA *nears edge of stage.* DILLINGER *grabs* KUCKTA, *punches him violently in the stomach. He falls in moaning pain to the floor.*

DILLINGER: I thought we decided everybody sits till they let Marcus out, huh? What are you, a traitor? I thought Marcus Sykowski was your friend? Now go sit down, traitor!

Pause.

DELORENZO: Hey, who ever figured skinny Dillinger for hitting Stanley?

O'CONNOR: Oh, but Stanley's mommy's so sick . . . Get out of here, punk!

Chorus of "yeahs."

LOUDSPEAKER: O.K., Stanley, I just sent Myles back.

KUCKTA (*crawling to* MARCUS) : Marcus, please let them send me out. My mother's sick . . .

MARCUS: Please stand up, Stanley . . .

KUCKTA: Marcus, you used to be a strong man, re-member!

MARCUS: Stanley, get up, please!

DELORENZO: Go home . . . get out of here, traitor!

O'CONNOR: Yeah, traitor, before we mess you up!

DILLINGER: Go on, you can come back tomorrow.

MARCUS: JoJo, I want you to let him out!

DELORENZO: Kid, let us handle it, O.K.?

MARCUS: But the poor guy's mother——

DELORENZO: Stanley, out of here 'fore I kick your face, understand! Now, blow!

KUCKTA (*to* MARCUS) : I hope everything works out for you, pitching friend.

KUCKTA *exits.*

DELORENZO: You've come to depend on people, kid. These are not the old days . . .

SHATTUCK: We're doing it all for you, kid . . .

LOUDSPEAKER: Kuckta, 73 and 40 then . . . it's your last chance . . .

O'CONNOR: Not here!

DELORENZO: So how's the wife doing with the acting?

MARCUS: Fine.

LOUDSPEAKER: Delorenzo, on 39 and 40. Let's go, everything's piling up out here!

KOLKOWSKI: Fats, we told you Sykowski goes out first or none of us move.

LOUDSPEAKER: But, he's only for nice and light, and everything out here's a trunk this morning!

DELORENZO: O.K., fats, let 'em sit.

Downstage left, RAINCOAT MAN *in shortsleeve shirt and slacks appears. His face is covered in Magic Marker.*

SHATTUCK: JoJo, who's he?

DILLINGER: JoJo, that's not Myles!

DELORENZO: Mister, you tell fats we're not budging!

MAN: Sykowski, that trick your wife pulled I didn't find funny.

MARCUS: I figured you'd be showing up soon.

MAN: Time's run out . . .

MARCUS: JoJo, I've got to go now . . .

DELORENZO: Kid, I don't like this. We're willing to give up going out so that you can——

MARCUS: Please don't anybody move. It's got to be done . . . (*Whispering to* MAN.) I'm glad you didn't wear your . . . raincoat. They would have recognized you for sure . . .

MAN: Things going to be extra rough 'cause of your wife's stunt, Sykowski!

MARCUS: It was only Magic Marker. Magic Marker washes off.

MARCUS *and* MAN *exit.*

DELORENZO: Maybe I was with the guy in the Army?

Rising, crossing downstage left, watching MARCUS *and* MAN *disappear.* OTHERS *moving downstage left, joining him.*

I know that face from someplace, but where . . . where? Listen, I'm going to follow them.

DELORENZO *disappears. Several seconds and* MAN *dressed exactly as* DELORENZO *returns to stage, back to* CADDIES.

O'CONNOR: JoJo, what's up?

MAN *turns and faces* CADDIES.

12

The War Has Been Resumed

Upstage right in a booth, elevated, glass enclosed, LEROY
STARR *with a* 2ND MAN, *adamant conversation, unheard.
Entire back wall of stage covered by bright white, movie-
like screen. Upstage left,* CANDY CANE *sits at white table
covered by microphones, sits profile left to the audience.
Several seconds, conversation in booth grows more
heated, then* TWO MEN *suddenly laughing, all still un-
heard. Several more seconds, then* . . .

MICROPHONED VOICE: Twenty seconds to show time . . .
  (*Pause.*) fifteen seconds to show time . . . (*Pause.*)
  ten, nine, eight, seven, six, five, four, three, two,
  one . . . On the air!

CANDY CANE (*into microphone, simultaneously huge picture of her, face front, projected on back wall of
  screen*) : At the recommendation of my many close
  friends, I have come on television to ask a favor of
  the people of Boston. I am Candy Cane Sykowski,
  wife of Marcus Sykowski, once pitching star of the
  Red Sox of Boston and, as you all must know, now
  taken by crippling disaster. But that is only minor
  tragedy to what befalls us this cold month of November. For these past five days Marcus and I, we to-

gether, have kept and lived with a secret, but we can no longer . . . can't go on. Our Junior, our eight-month-old son, has been kidnapped, has been taken from us and we plead your help. The police suspect a tie-in with my good husband's tragic maiming, but as Marcus is kept silent about the matter, as all you have read, we are left with only the cooperation of the citizenry of Boston's finest in resolving our heinous loss. (*Pause.*) Our Junior is very large for his age, can crawl adroitly, has eyes beautifully black like shined ebony buttons and hair . . . like me. He was last seen in the vicinity of Roxbury and St. James, last Sunday in early afternoon in a blue canopied carriage which I'm glad to report had the roof full up at the time because the rains this week have been frequent and mercilessly cold. As to any noticeable characteristics . . . oral sounds, birthmarks, etc. . . . . I can only add that——

Suddenly microphone sound cut, projection of CANDY CANE *replaced by* NEWSCASTER *who blares,* "News flash, news flash, news flash!" *He then adds, deeply solemn in tone:*

NEWSCASTER: From Washington, the President has just this minute announced that the war has been resumed, to repeat . . . the war has been resumed. This very hour twelve battalions are being dispatched hastily to the area of engagement. Please stay tuned to WNTZ for further——

Now suddenly, NEWSCASTER *projection fades from wall, whiteness.* LEROY STARR *and* 2ND MAN *in glass enclosed booth, heated words, gesticulations, un-heard,* CANDY CANE *sitting in silence; several seconds and* LEROY *suddenly turning to microphone in booth.*

LEROY STARR *(heard through speaker)* : Baby, you're do-ing beautiful, exquisite. Few seconds and you'll be back on . . .

CANDY CANE: Leroy, you sure I can't add a few words about Marcus' being missing too . . . ?

But LEROY STARR *has already gone back to argument with* 2ND MAN, *doesn't hear or see her; long pause of silence,* CANDY CANE *finally laying head on top of table.*

13
Winter Is the Final Season

Stage in darkness. Sounds of loud laughter. Several seconds, then the clicking sound of a slide projector. Onto back wall of stage, a picture is projected: that of a stage, bare and set-less, stagehands in motion, carrying flats, hammering nails. Oohs and aahs of characters on darkened stage in response to projection, then:

2ND WOMAN'S VOICE: Hey, isn't that Olivare with the black hammer there?

1ST WOMAN'S VOICE: Where's Olivare . . . where, where?

2ND WOMAN'S VOICE: There, there, it's him . . . swinging the black hammer!

1ST WOMAN'S VOICE: But where, where . . . it looks so bare!

2ND VOICE: There, there . . . with the shaggy hair!

1ST VOICE: Dear, you will take my fingertip and show me where . . .

Burst of mad laughter.

2ND VOICE: There, there, there! Can you see it now?

LEROY STARR: That is Olivare with the black hammer, isn't it?

1ST VOICE: There, now I see him . . . right there!

CROWD *claps at her achievement.*

85

. . . So amazing, seven weeks ago a stagehand and now he plays opposite our sweet Candy Cane in my Oscar's newest extravaganza! So, so exciting!

1ST MAN'S VOICE (*foreign accent*) : Starr, you will make slide to next picture, please! What the world needs now is controversy, controversy, controversy!

3RD WOMAN'S VOICE: Poor Oscar, it's no wonder you chase young things . . .

Back wall suddenly white and blank. In darkness, sound of slide projector.

LEROY STARR: Oscar, I'm changing the picture now.

Onto back wall, second slide. Picture of curtain call, costumed actors downstage on apron. Center of group, CANDY CANE *and handsome leading man (* OLI-VARE) , *red roses in arms, two faces wide with smiles.*

1ST WOMAN'S VOICE: There, there, that's Olivare next to Candy! He's so, so much easier to recognize in costume. It's him, it is, it is!

Cheering.

LEROY STARR: How's about a loud cheer for our two new stars . . . whataya say!

Cheering—Hip, Hip Hurray, Jolly Good Fellow, etc. Ends.

CANDY CANE: Thanks, everybody, we're very happy.

OLIVARE: We couldn't have done it without every one of you . . .

More cheering.

2ND MAN'S VOICE: So sweet. They've kept their modesty . . .

LEROY STARR: Friends, I'm sure our Oscar has something to add . . . isn't that right, partner?

More cheering.

1ST MAN'S VOICE: Listen, I pay the young ones for performing, controversy, controversy, to act, to make stars. They earn their money good, hah . . . good, good, good!

More cheering.

But to add . . . in all my years arranging plays——

Suddenly sounds, loud and angry, from street below. Crash of metal, car being overturned, spraying glass, woman's scream, chanting voices . . . in response, OSCAR raises voice:

Ja, in all my years arranging plays, have I never——

1ST WOMAN'S VOICE (*yelling over din*) : Oscar, wait until it passes. No one can hear you.

Chanting at height, clearly audible: "No more war, no more war!" Muffled sounds of exploding gasoline, "No more war!"

1ST MAN'S VOICE (*screaming*) : I wait until madness passes. No one can hear me!

Chanting pounds on, slow fade, then several loud screams topped by even louder cheers, chant dying. Long silence. No one moving.

87

OLIVARE'S VOICE: Don't they ever sleep?

3RD WOMAN'S VOICE: It's very late . . .

2ND WOMAN'S VOICE: The poor papers, again they won't be allowed to show pictures . . .

Pause.

1ST MAN'S VOICE: Craziness in our *schönsten* America, ach!

Pause.

1ST WOMAN'S VOICE: Oscar, was it so bad in the old days?

LEROY STARR (*laughing*): Oscar, I'm turning the lights back on. . . .

Stage is lighted. People seated about room. Sudden scream from 1ST WOMAN, pointed finger to upstage right where sits, with back to audience, MARCUS SYKOWSKI, tattered sport jacket, dirt-smeared. WOMAN screams again. MARCUS stands, turns slowly. His face covered by nylon stocking drawn tight. Right hand hidden behind breast front of coat. Stone silence. Then CANDY rises from chair.

1ST WOMAN (*nervously*): Dear, don't go near him . . . he has a gun.

1ST MAN: Would you like I call the police?

OLIVARE: I knew he wasn't dead.

CANDY CANE moves center stage, facing husband MARCUS.

1ST WOMAN: Don't! He has a gun!

MARCUS: Candy, pull the stocking off my head . . .

SHE *moves hesitatingly, stops.*

It's very tight . . .

Quickly, SHE *moves toward him,* HE *bending forward;* SHE *pulls off stocking.*

You thought my face would be mashed, didn't you?

Pause.

My face isn't mashed.

HE *steps, falling into her arms.* SHE, *having no choice, catches and holds him.*

I came up the fire escape. The bedroom's empty. Where's Junior?

CANDY CANE: Still with the lady, Miss Weitz.

MARCUS: But it's been over two months!

CANDY CANE: More like five hundred miles for me!

MARCUS: You weren't hard to find. You've become known, you're almost a star. I came up the fire escape. It's cold outside, famously cold for January, but I made it like a monkey . . . (*Laughing.*) Oh, my pitching arm's so strong, been lifting my weights every day . . . so, so goddamn strong. Gunna make it back big for sure! This is some place you've got— nice, but cold. Junior may not like it. We may just have to move!

CANDY CANE: Marcus, show me your hand under your coat . . .

MARCUS: I can't move it. You'll have to help me. (CANDY *does,* HE *revealing taped hand.*) It's my pinky. It's gone . . .

1ST WOMAN: Poor man, and I thought it was a gun!

MARCUS: Ladies and gentlemen, I apologize for——

Suddenly CANDY CANE *rushes stage right to desk, madly sorting through papers.* MARCUS *rushes to her.*

But I've come back. I've been away and now I'm back, back to make it big. Just the other day I got a baseball and tested and, no kiddin', I can grip it good as ever. Maybe my curve won't match Marichal of 'Frisco any more and——

CANDY CANE (*handing* MARCUS *envelope*) : It's for your arm piece. It's all there . . . Take it, you'll need it. (*Suddenly yelling.*) Okay, Leroy, whataya say we make some noise, huh, it's too quiet around here!

MARCUS: Oh don't you see I can't tell you . . . else they'd start chopping you up too!

CANDY CANE *makes sudden grab for* MARCUS, *hugging violently. Long pause of silence.*

CANDY CANE: All the time you were gone I wore my pedometer around my waist, just so I'd know, and today, I mean this morning, for the first time this morning, I forgot to pin it on. (*Crossing back to* OLIVARE.) You'll come visit me first time the Red Sox come North, won't you?

MARCUS (*smiling*) : Even if I have a glass eye and have to wear a rubber crotch? (*Extending hand to* CANDY CANE, *no response.*) Maybe I'll see you soon. (*Phone rings.*) Nobody move, please! (*Picks up phone.*) Hello, yes, yes, I'll be there as soon as I can . . .

Yes, I'm leaving now. (*Hanging up phone.*) Soon everything'll be good again . . .

CANDY CANE: Goodbye——

MARCUS: Nice meeting you people. And sorry I was so worked up when I came in. It was a long climb. (*Turning, catching sight of* OLIVARE, *crosses to him, extending bandaged hand.*) I don't think I caught your name?

OLIVARE, *rising, extends own hand, but suddenly* MARCUS *punches him in face, knocking him to the floor.* MARCUS *kisses* CANDY CANE *quickly on cheek, starts for door, wheels about.*

Baby, you won't believe me, but now I think I've gone and broken the knuckle too! (*Exits.*)

14

Fenway Park

Spotlight downstage center, shining upon baseball pitcher's mound, elevated 8–10 inches above stage floor. Several seconds, then voices from a distance in the dark.

MAN'S VOICE: Listen, why don't you go home 'fore you get frost bite? Now, how you gunna manage spring training you get frost bite, . . . answer me that!

MARCUS: I'm going to stand on the pitching mound and see if it's the right level.

MAN'S VOICE: But this is a January like no one ever saw, everything froze shut. People ain't even leaving their houses. Listen, get yourself a bottle and sit in a nice warm room where you belong, huh?

Short pause, sound of approaching feet. TWO MEN *now upstage left, but still in dark, from far away, vague sound of bus- or truck-like engines.*

MARCUS: Do you hear that? Listen, in the parking lots behind left field?

MAN: Kid, come on, it's only the city trucks come to sand the roads . . . Don't you have any idea how slippery it's gotten?

MARCUS (*laughing warmly*) : Only come to test the level of the mound, not even going to throw a ball and they pack 'em in buses, following me! Can you hear 'em, just to sit in the cold stands of winter and watch me walk over the field. Got to admit, it's something, really!

Engine sounds again, followed by voices.

There, can you hear 'em now?

MAN: Kid, whataya gone, marbles? That's only little kids dragging sleds across the lots. Listen, why don't you come back and have a cup of coffee with me . . . it's almost hot.

MARCUS: Isn't a ballpark overpowering the minute before it begins to fill, completely overpowering?

MAN: Begins to fill? Kid, it's winter . . . no one's around!

MARCUS: It's just like opening day'll be when I face the Yankees!

MAN: A year ago it was Teddy Kennedy and you and the hockey Bruins with Orr and Esposito, then mid-January and *Sports Illustrated* called you Atha-lete of the Year, after that February toward the end you was the first pitcher of Boston ever to sign——

MARCUS: Thanks for coming this far. I can go the rest of the way myself . . .

MAN: But don't you——

MARCUS: Listen, mister, you better get out of here.

MAN: Don't you——

MARCUS: Please go back!

MAN: The coffee's almost ready. (*Starting to exit.*) You'll have to come and have a cup.

Several seconds, sound of voices growing nearer.

MARCUS: Listen, do you hear? For sure, those aren't kids on sleds!

MARCUS now steps onto spotlighted mound. Engine sounds, voices growing louder. Facing downstage left, MARCUS places toe on pitching rubber, stretches arm, begins to make pitching motion toward imaginary homeplate offstage. Voices continuing to louden, children's screams: "Sykowski, Sykowski, burn it in there, mow 'em down . . ." etc. MARCUS, turning in place on mound, looking up into stands. Suddenly stadium-intense lights flood stage and audience. Up left, standing on top of a first-base bag, a tall rangy PLAYER, pounding his glove. He is dressed in Red Sox uniform.

MARCUS (*laughing loudly, looking at teammate*): George, it's a surprise for me, huh, like a birthday? (*Laughing on.*) You're beautiful, just beautiful . . . (*turning, facing audience, acknowledging second baseman, shortstop, etc.*) Tony C, me too, pal, me too! Hey Rico, here's the Yaz! Hey George, isn't that Mantle up there and Pepi on deck? You mean you got all the Yankees in on this too?

Crowd roaring on.

It's all for me, isn't it, even the fans!

From backstage, shout of "play ball" and ball softly thrown, MARCUS *catching it barehanded.*

Guess they want me to throw it, huh?

GEORGE (*pounding glove*): All I know is they brought us on buses, that's all . . .

Suddenly chrome arm, glove and Red Sox hat fly from offstage, landing near mound. MARCUS *comes off mound, picks them up, laughing.*

MARCUS: Guys have really gone the full boat, haven't you? It's almost beyond words . . . (*Trying to strap on arm, can't alone.*) George, give me a hand, will ya?

FIRST BASEMAN *crosses to him, helps him secure artificial limb.* MARCUS *hooks on glove, tugs cap firmly onto head, crosses back to mound. From backstage,* VOICE *barks, "Let's go, play ball!"* MARCUS *winds up and fires pitch.* VOICE *barking "ball one," pitch returned.* MARCUS *awkward with new limb, but at least knocks down throw.*

Gunna take a while to catch on, but the arm feels better than ever . . .

Fires second pitch, "Strike one." Ball returned, knocks it down, picks it up, fires again, "Strike two."

George, always trouble with Mantle before but watch this . . . (*Winding up.*) I finally got his number . . .

*Starting downward motion as shattering ring of rifle
fire heard.* MARCUS *abruptly stopping, grabbing face
with pitching hand, wobbling, turning toward audience. Blood flows in stream from between his eyes.
He rocks backward, then topples from mound onto
his face. Stadium lights dimming.*

MICROPHONED VOICE *(echoing about stadium)* : All Yankee
and Red Sox ballplayers return to the buses, now. Do
not go near Sykowski.

First baseman toward fallen MARCUS, *voice of in-
struction loudens.*

All Yankee and Red Sox ballplayers return to the
buses, now. Do not go near Sykowski.